ON SLIP RIGS AND SPIRITUAL GROWTH

POEMS BY TIMOTHY TARKELLY

OAC Books
Belle, Missouri
osageac.org

Copyright © Timothy Tarkelly, 2021
First edition 1 3 5 7 9 10 8 6 4 2
ISBN: 978-1-952411-67-0
LCCN: 2021942082

Author photos: Hilary Shepard
All rights reserved. No part of this publication may be reproduced or transmitted in any form or by any means, electronic or mechanical, including photocopying, recording or by info retrieval system, without prior written permission from the author.

Acknowledgments:

"The Charley Horse In Your Leg" and "Path Behind Mowat Lodge by Tom Thomson" first appeared in *Canoe Lake Memories* by Paddler Press.

"Catching Catfish With a Gourd By Jojetsu" first appeared in the July 2021 issue of *Rhodora Magazine*.

TABLE OF CONTENTS

A1A / 1
FIRST BROWN TROUT / 2
ON SLIP RIGS AND SPIRITUAL GROWTH / 3
PATH BEHIND MOWAT LODGE BY TOM THOMSON / 5
IMPROVED CLINCH KNOT AND A CIRCLE HOOK / 6
GALILEE / 7
THE GORGEOUS BASS PRO SHOP EMPLOYEE WHO DENIED MY CREDIT CARD APPLICATION AND GAVE ME TWO FREE HATS / 8
ETHICS I / 10
BEGINNER'S MIND / 11
DIAGNOSING THE PROBLEM / 12
HEMINGWAY TAKES ME FISHING / 13
STEELHEAD / 14
CATCHING CATFISH WITH A GOURD BY JOSETSU / 15
AT MONASTERY LAKE / 16
PINEDA BLUES / 17
HALF A MILE FROM THE VAN / 18
KNIFE POEM / 19
BOB CRUPI TAKES ME FISHING / 20

FISHING LESSONS / 21

THUS HAVE I HEARD / 22

TELESCOPIC ROD (AND OTHER THINGS YOU JUST
   CAN'T TRUST) / 23

ETHICS II / 25

THE CHARLEY HORSE IN YOUR LEG / 26

BOY FISHING BY WINSLOW HOMER / 28

JACK LONDON WOULD HATE YOU / 29

TAKE INVENTORY / 30

HOW DO YOU FISH FOR EELS? / 32

TIM EATS A BASS / 33

NEOSHO COUNTY STATE FISHING LAKE / 34

TO THOSE WHO LEAVE BEER CANS
   TO FLOAT DOWN THE RIVER / 35

THE BABY BLUEGILL SWALLOWS A HOOK / 36

SOMEONE TEACH ME TO FLY FISH / 37

THE HORSESHOE CRABS IN THE INDIAN RIVER
   OWE ME AN APOLOGY / 38

ROOSTER TAIL / 39

MELVILLE TAKES ME FISHING / 40

PINE PAVILLION NEAR A SPRING BY SHITAO / 41

ETHICS III / 42

ALARM SET FOR FOUR AM / 43

YAZOO / 44

DAYTONA BEACH PIER, 2002 / 45

TUNA FISHING BY SALVADOR DALI / 47

POSTCARD TO JASON BALDINGER / 48

ETHICS IV / 49

FISH-WITHIN-A-FISH, STERNBERG MUSEUM OF
   NATURAL HISTORY / 50

ANNABELLE CALLS ME OUT / 51

JOHNNY MORRIS TAKES ME FISHING / 52

NAMAZU / 53

TILAPIA / 54

IF YOU COULD GO FISHING WITH ANYONE,
   WHO WOULD IT BE? / 55

THOUGH IT MAY NOT SOUND
   LIKE REAL ADVICE / 57

To Bart Chaney
A giver of wisdom
A collector of years

The supreme good is like water,
which nourishes all things without trying to.
It is content with the low places that people disdain.

-Lao Tzu, *Tao Te Ching*

Wherever the river flows, everything will live.

-Ezekiel 47:9 CEB

A1A

No one's ever come home from Satellite Beach
without bruised heels
and a neck that could blush
a lobster into shame.
They got so much coquina rock
submerged in the sand,
there's almost no room to trip.
But we always find away.
Broken toenails, forgotten bait buckets
left dotted up and down
Florida's eastern coast.

FIRST BROWN TROUT

Pulled a whole earthen heart from the Pecos.
A refreshing brush with biology.
Something about order,
lineal banks
of satisfaction,
the sun's prerogative
to glimmer against
its dullest children.

ON SLIP RIGS AND SPIRITUAL GROWTH

It's ten degrees cooler
than I'd like, and the clouds have soured,
gone dark with a gentle, but inevitable fury.

Who am I to complain?
The pond is stocked and it would be greedy
to expect the sky to follow suit,
deliver its limits in suitable inches,
storms to be released once caught.

I'll leave if I need to,
but I'm not scared of the rain.
I've darkened so much myself,
soaked up a host of troubling questions,
daily frustrations, and the ever-present
laughter of a whole world that seems
to have figured it all out:
life itself mounted on the wall
for all to see.

I keep a patient eye
on my line. My chair isn't as old

as it is cheap, slumping in the mud,
steadily folding in,
but I need it to keep me up.
At least until the weather gives,
until I get what I came for.

There are no answers worth seeking
above the water's surface. I've got faith,
a whole leaden ounce worth,
stalking glory in the mud.

PATH BEHIND MOWAT LODGE BY TOM THOMSON

We carve words like "trailhead"
in the bark and pretend
that any path only goes one way.

Every traveler knows
when your joints thaw
and your boots have been washed
your past self falls
with the frost and mud.
You've seen things,
surmounted the crest
and breathed "by and by"
each time, calling two points home

and meaning it.

IMPROVED CLINCH KNOT AND A CIRCLE HOOK

You can find ferocity
in tidy things. Smooth
strength, a silver fistful
of meat. Just enough stretch
to set the hook on its own.

GALILEE

Simon Peter told them, *I 'm going fishing*. They said,
   We'll go with you.
They set out in a boat, but throughout the night they
   caught nothing.

                              -John 21:3 CEB

Fishermen have always been philosophers
Just ask Peter, shoulders strong
From hauling nets, feeding
Mouths that too often chew without tasting
Never stop to see the sea
As a delicate platter of waves
Waiting for a hand
To gently pluck purpose
From even the hardest to reach places

THE GORGEOUS BASS PRO SHOP EMPLOYEE WHO DENIED MY CREDIT CARD APPLICATION AND GAVE ME TWO FREE HATS

First, I'm sorry for noticing.
Failure will do that to you,
heighten your worst senses
to generate a more accurate picture,
the perfect snapshot of rejection.
Second, it pains me
to see myself how you must see me.
Barely a man, with an awkard smile
a credit score that feeds
with the pleco.
Forego the scripted congeniality,
the promise of more explanation in the mail.
Just kill me now, and set me up
with the stuffed fauna,
or set me free.
Click yes, click print,
and guide me to the sleeping bags
suited for all temperatures.
For what it's worth,
I would have used this money for good.

Real adventures, oiled with bear grease
and charted on antique maps.
While I can't stake the voyage on my own,
thanks for the few moments of your time,
for your warmth, for the free hats.

ETHICS I

Chuck says he'll be snagging
as long as there's life in the water.
Even then, he's bound to scrape up something
he's willing to fill his stomach with.
He'd just about set traps for baby deer,
pull its delicate hooves from the iron teeth,
throw it straight on the grill,
baste with butter, garlic, jam.
"No point in playin' pretty
with somethin' you're gonna chew up.
Throw its bones to the dog,
use the scraps for bait."

BEGINNER'S MIND

Out of my element,
my bag of tricks reduced
to only their painted, plastic forms.
It's silly when you think of it.
A tray of lures and a child's toy box
are no different, unless
in expert hands and employed
in the right conditions.
So I shrug off the ruse entirely.
Forget all outcomes.
Just enjoy watching
the bobber toss in the current.

DIAGNOSING THE PROBLEM

This preoccupation
with specifics,
latin names,
processes recorded with invisible ink
will only get you to the water,
maybe one or two drops
in the livewell.
Tie on some hope,
relax your eyes,
their swollen veins.
Cast in all directions.

HEMINGWAY TAKES ME FISHING

For Max and Dustin

A harpoon in one hand,
rum in the other,
a sea so calm,
he has to invent a tempest:
vague threats, worn-out tall tales
of cabin fever, murderers at high sea.
He gets angry that I'm not nervous,
as if he'd travel back alone
without anyone to hear
his tales of sweaty heroism.
I'm over old-man bravado
and its extended metaphors
about the threat of nameless death,
an inability to rise with the tide.

STEELHEAD

Moody complexion
All colors run together
Taken from its fierce beginnings
Instinctual surges in the comfort of an eddy
Have its strength melt away
Fresh blood, skin forged in cold water
Lifeless
In a pan of butter, so much butter

CATCHING CATFISH WITH A GOURD BY JOSETSU

Dexterous skill and a keen eye
for tradition
birthed in mud, in footprints
that trail the village's end,
connect us to the ashen world,
its collection of modest colors,
of breathing things.

AT MONASTERY LAKE

I read that yucca is edible
And have dreamed of little else since
A life that fades into the mountains
Goatlike, dirt and balance
Brave feet and flowers
That carry more grit than beauty
Descend only to take
What the water has to offer

PINEDA BLUES

Mosquitos are blasting Wagner,
swarming in the combat glow
of the propane lantern,
set too close to our cots.
We got up so early
to check the crab traps,
float into the dark
before the tide heads home.
Itchy isn't the right word.
I want to light the grill back up,
lay across the grates,
let the sores rise as ashes
to settle in the sand.
I'm tired,
but if the night has been good to us,
breakfast will be amazing.

HALF A MILE FROM THE VAN

A lesson I should have learned by now:
You only need the tackle
you choose not to bring,
or accidentally leave at home.
At least the trail is fresh,
more inviting
on the way back.

KNIFE POEM

I hate my fillet knife
and would prefer an ancient blade.
Jasper, or obsidian. Set into
a fistful of wood, bound
with flesh. Fat. Whatever the woods
are willing to provide.
Something steady, built
from hunger, dirty fingernails
programmed to find rhythm in necessity.
Sculpting tools unafraid of breaking,
that sing through their long jagged cut
up the belly, through the jaw.
This is dinner, coarse though it may be.
Thumb-gutted, cooked whole,
awaiting your hands,
their trace scent of the lake,
as you pick out the bones,
give thanks for clear water,
for your resourceful forebears,
for your forager's heart.

BOB CRUPI TAKES ME FISHING

Silent warrior,
bets the house on eight pound test.
Patience so deadly
it kills, brings all conversation
to a tightened stare,
thoughts as delicate
as swimmerets
or any part of a crawfish
that seems so mistakenly soft,
but keep the bass coming.

FISHING LESSONS

I cut my teeth in the St. Johns River,
a cane pole presenting
whatever I could squeeze onto an aberdeen hook
to impatiently slosh from here to there,
never giving time its due,
its proclivity for rewarding patience
over want's demanding hunger.
My dad says "they're just not bitin'"
and blames luck,
but clearly means maturity
will have to surface
before opportunity can strike.

THUS HAVE I HEARD

The pond is calm,
my breath has mastered itself,
humming the Heart Sutra,
trying not to pause for questions.
There either is or isn't bait left on my hook.
The line is out there, diving beneath surface,
but unmoving. Like a faithless servant
bowing for gravity alone.
I could reel it in to check,
but answers are always an interruption.
The pond is calm,
and that is no small thing.

TELESCOPIC ROD (AND OTHER THINGS YOU JUST CAN'T TRUST)

A sentry on the bank
firmly grasping his livelihood,
a pole he can take anywhere:
the remote river bend
out of reach to most people.

Here is a man who longs to be mobile,
spends his days dreaming of wild places
almost always encased in concrete,
bathing in fluorescent shame,
secretly plots to fit his whole life
in his vehicle, or even a backpack.

Breaks on the first cast.
A hook wedged in submerged rock,
a tug to work the gear loose,
an explosion. A fishing pole
torn to pieces and a bleeding hand
that's more surprised than hurt.

It's a long walk back,
and even on his good days,
this is always the worst part.
An engine comes to life,
sings its steady chorus of retreat.

ETHICS II

Fishing without a license
is like shopping without money.
Filling your cart
with as much meat as it can hold,
Expecting not to be charged on the way out,
telling the cashier you don't owe them anything.

THE CHARLEY HORSE IN YOUR LEG

Sometimes, you've earned it.
You've committed to
swinging to your eighth thistle, to
catching the elusive bass
you've only seen glimpses of.
Been on your feet for hours,
caught a hook in the meat
between your thumb and index finger,
blood dripping down your shirt and jeans.
Your head is still reeling
from when you slipped in the mud.
The heat is draining your stability.
Lunch is cooling somewhere. You thought
you'd be done by now and of course
the music of failure is rising in your ears,
in between waves of electric pain.
It's drowning out the blow-ups,
giving this disaster of a day a perfect soundtrack.
A throaty cello solo rises, taunting you,
interspersed with the voices of your life's hecklers,
like cymbal splashes, setting a tighter pace
for your heartbeat. Crying is just a function

of the body, like a thermometer, reminding us
just how badly we're doing at any given moment.
And you may or may not notice the Charley horse
in your leg perched against that rock
because just as you were about to give up,
you felt the tell-tale vibration in your pole,
something living has walked into your charade.
Your rubber worm has to fight the forces of nature.
As you reel and reel, as you're bleeding, sweating,
crying all over the place. You think maybe
there's no such thing as a good fisherman,
just someone who is willing to put up
with this much bullshit and as you hold
what was supposed to be your dinner,
you think "Why let something fight so hard
just to lose?" And you let him go.

BOY FISHING BY WINSLOW HOMER

Those who can't do, paint,
distribute weight
in whatever troublesome proportions
best heats their armchair passions.
I'd love to go there,
allow my gaze to get lost
in the melting tree line,
eyeing the bobber with passing interest,
just trying to catch some atmosphere,
beyond happy
to reel in anything that's willing.

JACK LONDON WOULD HATE YOU

You're fresh air adjacent at best.
We see your shoulders drop
in practiced relaxation,
taking in a world you'll never appreciate.
That smell is your own sunscreen,
propane cooking fires.

TAKE INVENTORY

Stop and note the weight of my pack
and what brings me here:
a granola bar and a landing net,
the sound of rushing water.

I come without ego, but a chest
that stands proud and runs deep,
ready to push my voice
into whatever stream it cares to.

For a sport I claim to love,
I spend so much time cursing,
damning the dropped pliers, the lost lures,
or the nearly intangible ghostlike body
of four pound test.

Let frustration float
as quickly out as in.
Be ready to give thanks
for every nibble, every splash,
each brush with life.

Stop and note the tension,
the towhee's persistent call,
the irony rushing through the rocks.

Capture and evasion,
two hopes running
in the same river at the same time.

HOW DO YOU FISH FOR EELS?

Same as anything else
That squirms in the mud for a living
Put something bleeding on a hook
And hope the beast takes risks

TIM EATS A BASS

First catch of the season.
No need to cry over surprise victories,
creel limits set by trophy hunters
who apparently don't have to pay for their own dinner.
If I'm being honest, I catch and release
ninety-nine percent of the time.
But my oven holds no secrets.
Just cooking smells,
emotional maturity,
an understanding that it was built for a reason.

NEOSHO COUNTY STATE FISHING LAKE

for Chase Reed

The sun would blind us
if the sweat hadn't already.
We blame ourselves
for the empty stringer.
We've taken the old man's advice,
who floated by and shouted
you'll never catch anything
that far from the bank.
The fact is,
our wishes notwithstanding,
all opportunity has long since fled
to the darkest shelf.
It's ninety-five degrees. It's noon.
And his wisdom didn't work, either.

TO THOSE WHO LEAVE BEER CANS
TO FLOAT DOWN THE RIVER

for Jason Ryberg

I hear y'all chanting America
Its vinyl colors stamped
On your bumpers
Flimsy arguments about tradition
Pulled from faded blueprints
The Virginian homes of dead men
It's almost as if you've forgotten
The name is attached
To a place
God carved these valleys
So the Osage could drink
So the Earth could carry water
To its children

THE BABY BLUEGILL SWALLOWS A HOOK

Cut the string and let it go,
recite the data:
a certain amount of fish
survive the odds.
Rust, muscular miracles
allow life to carry on as usual.
Watch as it takes off,
only to see it spiral,
land gently at the bottom.
Curse your high hopes
that got you out of bed so early
just to fumble, deliver needless death.
Shed a tear,
hope for hungry catfish.

SOMEONE TEACH ME TO FLY FISH

Fishing poles are like throwing axes.
Wind up and sound fury, wielding
Frankish biceps and studied strength.
I don't know how to unstring my joints,
let them careen on their own
feather-like finesse
that should live in my wrist like a spirit in the attic,
some forgotten dead relative
that barely touches the floorboard
as it moves on muscle memory
and restful horror.
And I get hung up on simple words
like gear ratio, reel tension,
or any amount of math
that takes the action out of my own deliberate hands.
But I can stand in all water,
letting silence wash over my empty basket
without a care in the world.

THE HORSESHOE CRABS IN THE INDIAN RIVER OWE ME AN APOLOGY

The serration of an afternoon
spent chucking mullet into the wind
and coming up empty.
If the fish aren't biting,
maybe it's because the kids
are playing in the water.
Stepping without looking,
planting their pioneer bodies
right where they don't belong.

ROOSTER TAIL

Y'all's problem is you're overthinking it,
acting like fish have unlocked our tackleboxes,
memorized the specs, and adjusted their movement accordingly.
Take a look at yourself. When was the last time
you chased an ice cream truck
because it resembled your native diet?
There's no reason for a human mind
to be lured, sent salivating and begging for more
by flash. By sprinkles and tin-can music.
But it works every time,
on us,
on them, too.

MELVILLE TAKES ME FISHING

> *Compass, quadrant and sextant contrive*
> *No farther tides ... High in the azure steeps*
> *Monody shall not wake the mariner.*
> *This fabulous shadow only the sea keeps.*
>
> -Hart Crane, "At Melville's Tomb

We sailed into the storm.

The waves breaking at the bow,
a chaotic attempt to chip away
at darkness.

We've been tossed everywhere,
the stars swirling above,
no landfall to even think of.

How will we find our way back?

The ocean's equivalent of a bump.
I'm almost sent starboard,
reaching for anything solid
to grab onto.

Forget about that, he shouts into the spray.
No one ever finds what they're looking for.

PINE PAVILLION NEAR A SPRING BY SHITAO

Imagine yourself as the pebble,
dropped from any height.
A birth occurs at the surface.
The loose embrace of immersion,
shedding of weight.
A dance akin to flight,
all its gentle possibilities.
Count until you hit the floor,
settle among the rest and open your eyes.
Look up,
watch as the next one falls.

ETHICS III

> *"To get fish by destroying a dam benefits you one time."*
>
> -Hanshan

Off Old Highway 50,
innovation is a heavy burden.
Madmen stoke their fevers
with dreams of fire,
a stick of dynamite,
and a fishing hole that beckons
bright lights and spring cleaning.
We don't spend enough time
acknowledging simple truths:
few people need a reason beyond
I just wanna see what happens.

ALARM SET FOR FOUR AM

He keeps his sowbelly dreams
pinned to his truck's visor.
Never knew a Saturday
he didn't greet at the shore.
Up before God,
grinning all knowledge
at the sun, too lazy
to ever keep up.

YAZOO

for Hilary Shepard

Autumn has kept us inside long enough.
We shed our sweaters and fill the car
with fuel, overnight bags.
We greet the gators in Mississippi
with camera flashes
and hearts newly shined by the mud.
Dare our troubles to come find us,
root us out of the south,
try to rob our lines of their spoils.
We'll be too far gone by then, knee-deep
in sweat tea, our voices morphing
into an unrecognizable shape.

DAYTONA BEACH PIER, 2002

I order a grouper sandwich,
count the livelihoods
tied to the railings.
Texture is everything.
The give of crisp to the teeth,
crunch, tenderness,
vinegar cutting through, stinging
its name into my palate,
leaving words I can only voice
in groans of delight.
The windows here aren't clean.
How could they be?
All the wind, the water,
the sea salt.
People are wearing rubber jackets,
in spite of the sun.
Shrimp nets emerge
like battle-worn oars,
ready to push out,
carry us home.

The hushpuppies alone
were worth the trip.
Pickled onions were a smart choice.
Tied it all together.

TUNA FISHING BY SALVADOR DALI

We savor the fight,
but deny the violence,
the splashing strokes of death,
the bones left to spike the sand
in increments that should astound.
If the sound of the ocean had a color:
blue, sure, but mostly the off-grey
sheen of carcasses left to season
on the shore.

POSTCARD TO JASON BALDINGER

Your appreciation for the prairies,
their flint-hewn heights
and astonishing breadth of amber growth
is well-grounded,
but on your next pass through Kansas,
visit the flatlands.
Sit on the bank of Big Creek,
its carp swirling in the silt,
its waters, once offered
as a drink to Custer's horses,
now the proving grounds
for lonely souls
to confront the summer heat
and listen to the orioles
as we try to pry meaning
from a harsh summer.

ETHICS IV

I'm careful to flatten
every barbed hook.
Target as you will,
but you never know what you'll catch by accident,
forced to return the too-young, the out-of-season
with a mouth mutilated by its indiscretion.
Or, god forbid,
let next spring's fresh lunch,
some rare native beauty,
die as a fingerling
in an attempt to prove
that you can outmaneuver nature's best minds,
that you're the final deliverer
of Mother Earth's consequences.

FISH-WITHIN-A-FISH, STERNBERG MUSEUM OF NATURAL HISTORY

Luck is a fickle beast
armed with ray fins
that rudder blind
through eons of muscular growth.
Imagine swallowing that much truth,
that all life has the potential
to end in a moment,
get hung as a monument
to cosmic indifference,
piscine tombs.

ANNABELLE CALLS ME OUT

It's true
My stomach is as taut
As a powerline in July
No stretch
Just a spineless dip toward the dirt
One hand, firmless
Holding the head to the stone
As I try to do anything
Worth doing with my knife
Crying over gleaned scales
Squirming bodies
That awful noise
Coming from some dead
Wet duct

JOHNNY MORRIS TAKES ME FISHING

We leave the lake cleaner than we found it.
Hearty plans await us. A large table.
fish stew, rich and red, waving its smoky flag
from little ceramic bowls.
Everyone is invited.
Over dinner, we talk technique,
where to point the rod when you're working
a top-water lure. He interrupts
to pepper in his roots, wisdom he's picked up:
"Family is everything."
"A good Missouri boy would never
leave their trash, their
broken rubber worms behind."
"This water gives life,
it's up to us to keep it that way."

NAMAZU

The Earth is neither kind nor unkind.

-Thich Nhat Hanh, *Love Letter to the Earth*

The bloodlines pump pure sludge down here,
where the warmth of the ground
begins.
Life boils
out of intentionless hunger.
We rarely recognize
Mother Earth's gentle touch
in such plainly painted work.
There's an impulse
to squeeze out danger,
to dive until our eyes bulge from the pressure,
fight the deep
with new solutions:
high tech hubris and a flashlight.
Instead, let's breathe,
accept destiny as it picks up our scent
and strikes, crumbling whole cities
in the process.

TILAPIA

Flavor, thy name is cursed.
Too many dinner guests
fooled by marketing,
gossip about fat content
wet with colonial pride
and barnacled ideas on
taxonomy.
Who are we
to rip the scales off anything,
let alone the treasure from
the disciples' own hooks, the paint
from Egypt's deepest walls,
the supplicant prayers of the hungry?
All things the sea submits to us
should be met with thanksgiving.

IF YOU COULD GO FISHING WITH ANYONE, WHO WOULD IT BE?

Your grandfather, pried from his pine box
to walk to Earth once more, heads right
to the marina, picks you up on the way.
A tournament favorite,
an array of glowing screens,
buttons you fear may connect
to some essential function
of the USS Enterprise.
Some earlier version of your uncle, brother,
or whoever dragged you to the river
before you were old enough
to appreciate dawn's opportune shores.
Tobit could offer his accidental expertise,
the promise of doting angels
and their strict health codes.
Ahab, his wild ideas about success,
his penchant for longwinded dinners.
Or me,
a man who is always just doing his best,

refusing to give in
and buy a baitcaster,
forever whistling predictable tunes,
the mechanical jingle of a Zebco.

THOUGH IT MAY NOT SOUND LIKE REAL ADVICE

There is no way
to fish the current,
fishing the current
is the way.

Timothy Tarkelly's work has appeared in Unstamatic, *Back Patio Press, Jupiter Review, The Daily Drunk,* and more. He has two previous collections of poetry published by Spartan Press: *Luckhound* (2020) and *Gently in Manner, Strongly in Deed: Poems on Eisenhower* (2019). When he's not writing, he teaches in Southeast Kansas.

This project was made possible, in part, by generous support from the Osage Arts Community.

Osage Arts Community provides temporary time, space and support for the creation of new artistic works in a retreat format, serving creative people of all kinds — visual artists, composers, poets, fiction and nonfiction writers. Located on a 152-acre farm in an isolated rural mountainside setting in Central Missouri and bordered by ¾ of a mile of the Gasconade River, OAC provides residencies to those working alone, as well as welcoming collaborative teams, offering living space and workspace in a country environment to emerging and mid-career artists. For more information, visit us at www.osageac.org

www.ingramcontent.com/pod-product-compliance
Lightning Source LLC
Chambersburg PA
CBHW030351100526
44592CB00010B/910